It Starts With Food Cookbook

The Low Sugar Gluten-Free &
Whole Food CookBook

40 Delicious & Healthy Recipes
Your Family Will Love!

Perfect For Those Following
"The Whole 30®" Program

by

New Health CookBooks

Whole 30 is a registered trademark of Whole9 Life LLC

COPYRIGHT

DISCLAIMER

Contents

Contents

Preface

It Starts With Food by Dallas and Melissa Hartwig was named one of the top 50 health books by the Huffington Post in September 2012, and for a good reason; this book is responsible for changing the lives of its readers. If you have not read it yet, we highly recommend that you do. There is a link to the kindle version in section 6.

Those who choose to apply the program laid out in the book have reported the elimination of a wide variety of symptoms, diseases and ailments in just 30 days. Here is a list of just some of the symptoms people have reported relief from:

diabetes · high cholesterol · high blood pressure · obesity · acne · eczema · psoriasis · hives asthma · allergies · sinus infections · migraines · acid reflux · celiac disease · Crohn's · IBS bipolar disorder · depression · seasonal affective disorder · eating disorders · ADHD endometriosis · PCOS · infertility · arthritis · Lyme disease · hypothyroidism · fibromyalgia

We designed this cookbook to support those who are on the "It Starts With Food Whole 30®" program, and for anyone who believes in the benefits of eating whole foods and avoiding processed foods and sugars. We hope you enjoy these recipes as much as we do!

New Health CookBooks

Reminder...

Since you are eating what the animals in your meal ate, when choosing your meats, you should select free-range, hormone-free chicken and turkey, grass-fed beef, pasture-fed pork and wild cold-water fish.

On The "It Starts With Food" Diet?

If you are on the It Starts With Food Diet Program, almost all of these recipes are appropriate for everyone. Some of the recipes contain a note indicating that you must be tolerant of dairy, eggs, or gluten-free grains.

Chapter 1

Breakfast

Start Your Day Right

Almond-Flour Hotcakes

*A great alternative for those craving traditional refined-carb pancakes, these delicious griddle cakes need to be cooked on low heat as they burn easily. For those who can tolerate **nuts** and **eggs.***

Serves: 2

Ingredients:

1 cup organic almond flour

1/2 cup organic applesauce, unsweetened (homemade if possible)

1 tablespoon pulverized coconut (coconut flour)

2 organic, cage-free eggs

1/4 cup soda water

1/4 teaspoon cinnamon

1/4 teaspoon nutmeg

1/4 teaspoon salt

Clarified butter (for cooking and serving)

Strawberries, raspberries and blueberries (for serving, if desired)

Preparation

In a large mixing bowl, thoroughly combine all ingredients through salt.

Over low heat in a large skillet or on a griddle pan, melt a small amount of butter. Spoon batter onto skillet or griddle; spread if needed to form a 1/4 inch hotcake.

Cook until bubbles appear on the surface; flip and continue cooking until cooked through and golden brown.

Repeat as necessary with remaining batter; serve hot and with clarified butter and berries if desired.

Garlic-Spinach Vegetable Skillet Frittata

*Hearty and satisfying, this ideal weekend brush dish can also be served for dinner! For those who can tolerate **dairy** and **eggs**.*

Serves: 4

Ingredients:

1 pound organic spinach leaves, washed, chopped and wilted (see note)

9 organic, cage-free eggs

2 tablespoons organic milk

1/3 cup freshly grated Parmesan cheese (not jarred)

2 tablespoons chopped sun-dried tomatoes (dry or jarred in oil) (see note)

1/4 cup organic red bell pepper, chopped

1/4 cup fresh organic basil leaves, chopped

Sea salt (to taste)

Freshly cracked black pepper (to taste)

1 tablespoon organic olive oil, extra-virgin

1 cup chopped red onion

1 to 2 cloves fresh garlic, minced

3 ounces cream cheese, softened (see note)

1 tablespoon snipped fresh chives, optional

Preparation

Preheat oven to 400 degrees.

In a large bowl, thoroughly combine eggs, milk, Parmesan, tomatoes, peppers, basil, salt and pepper. Set aside.

In a large oven-proof skillet over medium heat, cook onion in olive oil until tender and translucent; approximately 5 minutes. Add garlic and cook 1 minute more. Add wilted spinach and thoroughly combine in skillet.

Pour egg mixture over spinach mixture and gently combine both mixtures. Drop teaspoonfuls of cream cheese atop frittata. Continue cooking until eggs are approximately half-set.

Place skillet into oven; bake approximately 15 minutes or until frittata is fully set and cooked through (160 degrees). Sprinkle each serving with fresh chives, if desired.

Notes:

To wilt spinach, place in a microwave-safe dish, partially cover with 1/4 cup water and cook on high until leaves wilt, watching carefully to prevent over-cooking.

Organically-farmed goat cheese can be used in place of cream cheese.

Classic Diner Steak-and-Eggs

*A time-honored favorite, this simple breakfast is filled with responsibly-farmed ingredients and sure to satisfy even the heartiest appetites! Preheating your skillet delivers restaurant-quality seared steaks. For those who can tolerate **eggs**.*

Serves: 4

Ingredients:

1 tablespoon canola oil

1 pound organic, grass-fed steak, approximately 1 inch thick

Sea salt to taste

Freshly cracked black pepper

2 tablespoons clarified butter

8 large organic, cage-free eggs

Preparation

Preheat your oven to 400 degrees.

Over medium heat, preheat a cast-iron skillet for approximately 5 minutes. Season your steak with sea salt and pepper. Add canola oil to skillet; increase heat to high and add steaks. Cook for approximately 4 minutes per side.

Transfer skillet to oven and cook until desired doneness is reached (see note). After cooking, allow steak to 'rest' approximately 10 minutes in order to prevent loss of natural juices.

In the meantime, heat 2 skillets over medium heat (or work in batches). In each, melt 1 tablespoon butter. Add eggs, stir with a fork and cook, uncovered, approximately 3 1/2 minutes. Cover and cook an additional 2 minutes or until done (160 degrees). Portion among 4 plates.

Slice your steak and divide among prepared plates.

Notes:

Follow these guidelines for perfectly cooked steak using an instant-read meat thermometer:

Medium: 145 degrees

Medium-Well: 155 degrees

Well-Done: 170 degrees

As with most recipes using beef, bison (buffalo) can easily be substituted. Bison is a great alternative due to its similar appearance and texture. In addition, nearly all US bison are responsibly raised, leading to less confusion at the supermarket.

Vegetable-Sausage Scramble

Use common sense when purchasing sausage – be sure you can pronounce all ingredients on the label and avoid any products containing MSG, sulfites or carrageenan. Due to high fat content, stick with organic sausage to avoid the potential toxins in industrially-raised animal fats. For those who can tolerate **eggs**.

Serves: 4

Ingredients:

6 large organic, cage-free eggs

1 teaspoon all-natural Cajun seasoning blend

1/4 teaspoon sea salt

2 tablespoons organic, lightly-flavored olive oil

2 teaspoons butter, unsalted, clarified

1 pound sausage, crumbled

1/4 cup chopped fresh red bell pepper

1/4 cup chopped fresh green bell pepper

1/2 cup shredded pepper-jack cheese

1 cup organic, no-sugar-added salsa (optional)

1/4 cup snipped fresh scallions (optional)

Preparation

In a mixing bowl, whisk together eggs, Cajun seasoning and sea salt. Set aside.

In a skillet over medium heat, cook sausage in olive oil and butter until no longer pink; add peppers and cook until crisp-tender, approximately 1 minute.

Add egg mixture to skillet and cook, stirring as needed, until eggs are set and cooked through (160 degrees). Sprinkle cheese on top and let stand until melted.

Portion eggs between four plates; garnish with salsa and scallions if desired.

Crustless Taco Chicken Quiche

*Zesty and hearty, this crust-free quiche is an easier and healthier alternative to refined-carb crusts. For those who can tolerate **dairy** and **eggs**.*

Serves: 8

Ingredients:

4 organic, cage-free eggs

1 cup organic milk

3 cups cooked, shredded chicken, organic, free-range

2 cups shredded cheddar OR pepper-jack cheese

1 cup prepared salsa (organic, all-natural)

1 (4.5 ounces) can chopped green chiles, drained

Sea salt and freshly cracked black pepper (optional)

Sour cream (organic, optional)

Additional salsa (optional)

Preparation

Preheat your oven to 350 degrees. Lightly grease a 9-inch pie pan.

In a mixing bowl, thoroughly whisk together eggs and milk. Add the chicken, salsa, chiles, salt and pepper (if desired); combine well.

Pour into prepared pie pan. Bake for 50 to 55 minutes or until completely cooked through (160 degrees) and set. Serve with sour cream and salsa, if desired.

Steaks with Sweet-Potato Hash

Decadent and satisfying, this breakfast treat is an excellent dairy- and egg-free option.

Serves: 4

Ingredients:

4 organic, grass-fed sirloin steaks, approximately 1 ½ inches thick (2 pounds)

Sea salt and freshly-cracked black pepper to taste

1 clove garlic, sliced very thin

2 large sweet potatoes, peeled and grated/shredded

1/4 teaspoon sea salt

1/4 teaspoon freshly-cracked black pepper

1/2 cup organic red bell pepper, diced

1/4 teaspoon garlic powder

1/4 teaspoon smoked paprika

1/8 teaspoon crushed red pepper flakes

2 tablespoons diced onion

3 tablespoons clarified butter

Preparation

Preheat your broiler. Rub steaks with salt and pepper as desired. Cut very small slits in steak fat and stuff a piece of garlic into eat slit. Place approximately 3 inches from heat and broil until desired temperature is reached (see note) flipping halfway through cooking time.

In the meantime, combine sweet potatoes, salt, pepper, onion powder, garlic powder, paprika and red pepper flakes. Heat a large, nonstick skillet over medium heat; add clarified butter.

In butter, saute red bell peppers and onion for 1 minute. Add sweet potato mixture and toss to coat with butter (add more butter if mixture appears very dry). Continue to toss and stir-fry approximately 3 minutes or until you begin to see browned bits. Cover skillet and cook for 3 to 5 minutes more, checking every minute, until potatoes are cooked through, tender and browned at edges.

Portion hash between 4 plates. Top each serving with a broiled steak.

Notes: Steak Times and Temperatures:
Medium Rare: 6 to 8 minutes per side; 145 degrees
Medium: 7 to 10 minutes per side; 155 degrees
Well-Done: 10 to 13 minutes per side; 170 degrees

If tolerable, a fried or poached egg can be added to each serving OR substituted for steaks.

Sweet Potato Pancakes

Savory and hearty, these potato cakes are an ideal breakfast side or light breakfast for those who can tolerate gluten free grains.

Serves: 4 (2 pancakes each)

Ingredients:

4 tablespoons flax seed powder

6 tablespoons water

2 large organic sweet potatoes, peeled and grated

1/2 cup organic sweet red bell pepper, diced

3/4 cup onion, diced or grated

1 teaspoon sea salt

1/2 teaspoon freshly-cracked black pepper

Clarified butter or olive oil for frying

1 cup unsweetened applesauce

Preparation

In a bowl, thoroughly combine flax seed powder and water. Whisk until mixture thickens (this is your egg substitute).

Squeeze sweet potato and onion between paper towels to remove as much excess moisture as possible. Combine with red bell pepper, flax mixture, salt and pepper.

Shape the potato mixture into four patties. Over medium heat, fry patties in butter or olive oil until golden brown, crisped and cooked through.

Serve pancakes with 1/4 cup of unsweetened applesauce on the side.

Note:

If making a larger batch of pancakes, keep cooked cakes warm in a low (200 degree) oven until ready to serve.

Banana Griddle Cakes

*Yet another way to satisfy your cravings without turning to refined flours or gluten, these two-ingredient wonders are a kid-pleasing family favorite! For those who can tolerate **eggs**.*

Serves: 2 to 4, depending on serving size

Ingredients:

4 organic, cage-free eggs

2 ripe bananas, peeled and mashed

Clarified butter (cooking and serving)

Fresh organic berries (for serving)

Preparation

In a bowl, thoroughly combine eggs and bananas.

Heat a heavy skillet or griddle pan over medium-low heat. Melt butter and pour batter onto griddle.

Cook until bubbles form and edges begin to brown (time depends on size of griddle cake).

Flip and continue cooking until cooked through and golden brown.

Serve topped with clarified butter and fresh berries, if desired.

Chapter 2

Lunch

Delicious Lunches

Herbed Salmon Salad

Packed with healthy omega-3s, wild-caught salmon is a wonderful fish choice. This light, fresh-tasting salad is an ideal option for light lunches or picnic parties!

Serves: 4

Ingredients:

1 1/2 cups chopped fresh organic celery

1/2 cup finely chopped red onion

1 tablespoon capers, drained and minced

Juice of 1 fresh lemon

1 tablespoon extra-virgin olive oil

2 tablespoons organic fresh basil leaves, chopped

1 tablespoon organic fresh dill, finely chopped

1/2 teaspoon dried thyme, crushed

1 pound wild-caught salmon, cooked, flaked into bite-size pieces

Sea salt and freshly cracked black pepper, to taste

Preparation

In a mixing bowl, combine first 8 ingredients; toss to coat. Gently stir in salmon pieces to coat, being careful not to break them apart. Taste and add salt and pepper as desired.

Keep refrigerated and serve chilled .

Notes:

If fresh salmon is unavailable, you may substitute canned salmon as long as the label clearly states that the fish was wild-caught

Sweet-Potato Salad with Pork

Smoky, southwestern flavors go deliciously well with sweet potatoes. Adding cooked and shredded pork turns this lighter salad into hearty main-dish fare! Using homemade olive-oil mayonnaise avoids the HFCS found in commercially-prepared varieties. For those who can tolerate eggs.

Serves: 10

Ingredients:

2 cups homemade olive-oil mayo (see Recipe and Food-Safety Warning)

1 teaspoon smoked paprika

1/2 teaspoon ground cumin

1/4 teaspoon crushed red pepper flakes

3 pounds organic sweet potatoes, peeled, cooked and cubed

2 cups shredded cooked pork, organic

1/2 cup chopped organic red bell pepper

1/2 cup chopped organic green bell pepper

1/2 cup diced red onion

Sea salt and freshly cracked black pepper, to taste,

Preparation

In a bowl, combine olive-oil mayo, smoked paprika, cumin and red pepper flakes. Add sweet potatoes, pork, peppers and onion. Gently stir and toss to coat. Taste; season with salt and pepper as desired.

Chill salad for at least 1 hour prior to serving.

Olive Oil Mayo:

Due to the potential presence of harmful bacteria, use caution when eating uncooked egg products. They should be used immediately and not be given to the elderly, children, or those with compromised immune systems. Pasteurized liquid eggs are a great alternative.

Ingredients:

Organic, cage-free pasteurized liquid eggs equivalent to 2 large eggs

2 cups organic light olive oil

Juice of one freshly squeezed lemon

1 teaspoon water

Preparation

Beat eggs and lemon juice and water until combined. In a bowl (using a whisk) or in a food processor, process yolk mixture and drip or (very) slowly pour in oil, continuously processing or whisking, until oil is gone and a thick, emulsified texture is achieved.

Greek Patty Melts

Satisfying and a delicious twist on the traditional burger, these fresh-tasting patties are bursting with Mediterranean flavor! For those who can tolerate **dairy**.

Serves: 4

Ingredients:

1 pound organic, cage-free ground turkey

1 teaspoon garlic powder

1 tablespoon clarified butter

4 large, sturdy lettuce leaves, organic, washed and patted dry

1 cup crumbled feta cheese

1/2 cup sliced and pitted Kalamata olives

1/4 cup snipped fresh dill

1/4 cup snipped fresh mint leaves

Preparation

Combine ground turkey and garlic powder. Using your hands, form ground turkey into 4 (1/4 pound) patties.

In a skillet over medium heat, place butter and cook patties, turning once, until no pink remains and turkey is done (165 degrees). Do not under-cook.

Assemble your burgers by placing each patty on a lettuce leaf. Top with feta, olives, dill and mint. Wrap up lettuce to create a packet.

Note:

*Organic ground lamb may be substituted for turkey for even more authentic Greek flavor. Cook ground lamb to **160 degrees**.*

If you can't find or don't like feta cheese, any good-quality crumbled blue cheese may be substituted.

Baked Sweet Potatoes with Ranch Dressing

*Ideal as a light lunch or dinner side! For those who can tolerate **eggs**.*

Serves: 4

Ingredients:

4 large, organic sweet potatoes, scrubbed

1 cup homemade olive-oil mayo (see recipe for Sweet Potato Salad with Pork)

1 cup organic canned coconut milk

1/4 teaspoon sea salt

1/2 teaspoon freshly cracked black pepper

1 1/2 teaspoons garlic powder

1/4 cup organic fresh dill, minced

4 tablespoons clarified butter, optional

Preparation

Preheat your oven to 400 degrees. Prick each potato skin with a fork several times to allow for steam venting. Place on a baking sheet and cook for approximately 50 minutes or until tender.

While sweet potatoes are baking, place dressing ingredients in a medium mixing bowl and thoroughly whisk together.

When sweet potatoes have cooled enough to handle safely, cut a slit in the top of each potato. Top with butter, if desired.

Serve either topped with ranch dressing or with dressing on the side.

Build-A-Box Cold Lunch

*Great for packing school or work lunches, this do-it-yourself collection of healthy ideas allows you to create your own personalized lunchbox! Choose 3 to 5 options from those listed below, making sure to create a balanced combination of fiber and protein. Some options are suitable for those who can tolerate **dairy**, **eggs** and **nuts**.*

Serves: Varies

Ingredients:

Organic Produce (see Note):

Apple slices

Pear slices

Peach slices

Grapes

Cherry or Grape Tomatoes

Orange sections

Celery sticks

Baby spinach leaves

Baby carrots

Broccoli florets

Cauliflower florets

Purchased or homemade items, organic:

Raisins (see Note)

Dried cranberries

Dried cherries

Dried fruit slices (apples, bananas)

Olives (pitted) (green, black, Kalamata, artisanal stuffed)

Nut butters (cashew, almond, macadamia)

Deli meat (roast beef, turkey, chicken)

Quick Cold Salads:

Salmon salad made with olive-oil mayo (see Note)

Tuna salad made with olive-oil mayo (see Note)

Cucumber or Zucchini "sandwiches" (see Note)

(Notes continued on next page)

Notes:

Properly wash all fresh produce

Dried fruits are great sprinkled atop celery slices spread with nut butter)

Choose deli meats with no MSG, sulfites or carrageenan

For an olive-oil mayo recipe, see recipe for Sweet Potato Salad with Pork)

Build "sandwiches" by stacking cold tuna or salmon salad between two cucumber slices

Important: *For safety, invest in an insulated lunch box or bag, and include a long-lasting ice pack with every lunch.*

Classic Chef's Salad

*Light yet satisfying, this classic favorite is a great way to use up leftovers! For those who can tolerate **dairy**.* Serves: 4

Ingredients:

1 pound baby mixed salad greens (arugula, romaine), washed and patted dry

1 pound baby spinach leaves, washed and patted dry

1 cup organic, free-range meat (chicken, turkey, pork, lamb, beef), cooked, cubed

1 cup shredded cheddar cheese

2 organic, cage-free eggs, hard-boiled and cubed

10 organic cherry or grape tomatoes, cut in half

1/2 cup organic red bell pepper strips

1/2 cup organic green bell pepper strips

1/2 cup homemade or natural, no-sugar-added dressing of your choice

In a large mixing bowl, combine greens.

Preparation

On four plates, arrange greens. Top with remaining ingredients except for dressing; serve with dressing on the side.

Better-For-You Caesar Salad with Chicken

*Traditional Caesar Salad comes packed with unhealthy croutons. This version leaves them out entirely, leaving all the flavor you love without the refined carbs! For those who can tolerate **dairy** and **eggs**.*

Serves: 4

Ingredients:

4 cups organic, fresh baby romaine lettuce, washed and dried, coarsely torn

1 cup olive-oil mayo (for recipe, see Sweet Potato Salad with Pork)

1/4 cup freshly grated Parmesan cheese (see Note)

3 cloves fresh garlic, finely minced

1 1/2 teaspoons freshly cracked black pepper

1/4 teaspoon dried basil, crushed

1/4 teaspoon dried thyme, crushed

1/4 teaspoon dried oregano, crushed

4 wild-caught anchovies, diced

1 1/2 cups organic, free-range chicken, cooked, cubed or shredded

4 wedges fresh lemon

Preparation

Arrange the romaine on 4 serving plates.

In a bowl, whisk together olive-oil mayo, Parmesan, garlic, pepper, basil, thyme and oregano.

Top romaine with chicken. Sprinkle each plate with diced anchovies; drizzle dressing over top. Serve with individual lemon wedges; squeeze over salads.

Note:

For those who can't tolerate dairy, this dressing can be made without Parmesan cheese. Keep in mind that the flavor will be different from a "traditional" Caesar salad.

Italian Grilled Chicken Breasts with Tomato Dressing

This quick chicken dish is bursting with fresh Italian taste. During the warmer parts of the year, use a traditional grill for even more grilled flavor!

Serves: 4

Ingredients:

4 organic, free-range chicken breasts

1 tablespoon extra-virgin olive oil

Sea salt and freshly cracked black pepper to taste

1 (14.5 ounce) can organic diced tomatoes, undrained

2 cloves fresh garlic, minced

1 tablespoon fresh basil, chopped

1 tablespoon fresh rosemary, chopped

1 tablespoon fresh oregano, chopped

1/2 teaspoon red pepper flakes, crushed

1/2 teaspoon onion powder

4 cups organic baby spinach leaves, washed and patted dry

Preparation

Preheat your grill pan over medium heat (see Note).

Place chicken breast halves in a plastic bag, seal and pound with a meat mallet until uniformly 3/4 inch thick. Discard bag. Brush the chicken with olive oil; season to taste with sea salt and pepper.

In a saucepan, combine tomatoes, garlic, basil, rosemary, oregano, red pepper flakes and onion powder. Bring to a simmer and cook 5 minutes.

Place flattened chicken breasts on grill pan, working in batches if necessary. Cook approximately 5 minutes per side, until no pink remains and internal temperature reaches 160 degrees.

Divide the spinach between four places. Top each with a grilled chicken breast; spoon tomato sauce over each.

Note:

To test the heat of a grill pan, let a drop of water fall onto the cooking surface. If the water sizzles, your grill pan is ready to cook.

Chapter 3

Dinner

Great Tastes

Sicilian Chicken alla Norma with Blood Orange Salad

Pasta alla Norma is one of Sicily's most famous dishes. This better-for-you version does away with unhealthy refined carbohydrates and adds extra protein and vegetables! Serves: 4

Ingredients:

4 organic, cage-free, boneless, skinless chicken breasts, pounded 3/4 inch thick (see Note)

1 tablespoon extra-virgin olive oil

1 (14.5 ounce) can organic diced tomatoes, undrained

3 cloves fresh garlic, minced

1/2 cup organic fresh basil leaves, coarsely chopped

1/2 teaspoon dried oregano, crushed

1 large organic eggplant, washed, cut into 1/2 inch thick slices

Clarified butter or olive oil, for sautéing

4 organic blood oranges, peeled, segmented and sliced

4 cups organic baby spinach leaves, washed and patted dry

1 1/2 cups sliced organic strawberries

1/2 cup homemade or purchased organic, no-sugar-added Italian vinaigrette

Preparation

In a skillet over medium heat, sauté chicken breasts in olive oil until no longer pink and cooked through (160 degrees); approximately 7 to 8 minutes per side.

In a saucepan, combine undrained tomatoes, garlic, basil and oregano. Bring to a simmer and cook for 5 minutes.

In another large skillet over medium heat, sauté eggplant slices in butter or olive oil until tender, approximately 5 to 7 minutes per side. Plate each chicken breast alongside fried eggplant slices; top both with tomato sauce.

Divide spinach leaves among 4 plates. Top with orange slices and strawberries; drizzle on vinaigrette.

Note:

To minimize mess and the potential for cross-contamination, place chicken in a heavy, zippered plastic bag and pound with a meat mallet or the bottom of a heavy skillet.

Special-Occasion Herbed Rack of Lamb

Surprisingly easy to make, this dish makes an impressive holiday display. To round out your meal, steam a mixture of fresh, seasonal vegetables and toss with butter or olive oil.

Serves: 8 (1 double-chop per serving)

Ingredients:

2 organic, free-range "frenched" racks of lamb (1 1/2 pounds and 8 ribs each) (see Note)

1 teaspoon sea salt

3/4 teaspoon freshly cracked black pepper

1 teaspoon organic light-flavored olive oil

4 cloves fresh garlic, minced

1 clove fresh garlic, cut into slivers

Sea salt and freshly cracked black pepper to taste

1 tablespoon snipped fresh organic thyme

1/4 cup fresh organic parsley, chopped

2 tablespoons snipped fresh organic rosemary

1 1/2 tablespoons organic extra-virgin olive oil

Preparation

Preheat your oven to 350 degrees; place a roasting rack inside a 13x9 inch roasting pan.

Over high heat, preheat a large, heavy skillet for at least 2 minutes. Pat your lamb dry and rub with salt and pepper. Add olive oil and brown lamb (all sides) until golden, approximately 10 minutes per rack.

In a small bowl, combine garlic, salt and pepper as desired, thyme, parsley, rosemary and olive oil. Cut small slits into lamb; insert garlic slivers. Rub mixture onto browned lamb, patting and pressing as needed so that mixture coats the lamb.

Place racks in prepared pan; roast, uncovered, for 15 minutes. Cover racks loosely with aluminum foil: roast an additional 50 to 60 minutes or until done (see Note for cooking times).

Serve alongside vegetables.

Note:

"Frenching" is a method of trimming lamb; your butcher will be able to do this for you.

Using an instant-read meat thermometer, the following times will ensure perfect doneness:

Medium-Rare: 145 degrees; Medium: 160 degrees; Well-Done: 170 degrees and up

Slow Cooker Beef Stew with Mushrooms and Root Vegetables

Ideal for chilly days, this hearty and satisfying stew saves you time and eliminates the HFCS in canned tomato paste. You may leave the tomato paste out if you don't have time to make your own; the tomato flavor will be less intense.

Serves: 6

Ingredients:

Light-flavored olive oil (for greasing slow-cooker)

1/2 cup chopped red onion

1 cup organic carrots, peeled and cut into 1 1/2 inch pieces

2 cups fresh, organic sliced celery

1 pound parsnips, peeled and cut into 1 1/2 inch pieces

2 pounds organic, free-range beef stew meat, cut into 1 1/2 inch pieces

1 (14.5 ounce) can diced tomatoes, undrained

3/4 cup homemade beef stock or water

Sea salt and freshly cracked black pepper to taste

3/4 cup homemade tomato paste (optional) (see note)

2 tablespoons snipped fresh organic thyme

Preparation

Grease your slow-cooker using olive oil. Layer (don't mix) onion, carrots, celery, parsnips and, last, stew meat. Pour diced tomatoes and stock (or water) over layered mixture. Add salt and pepper as desired. Set slow-cooler temperature to Low; cover and cook for 8 to 12 hours (see Note) or until vegetables and meat are cooked through and tender.

Add tomato paste and snipped thyme. Increase heat to High; cover and cook for 10 minutes.

Note:

To prepare homemade tomato paste for this recipe, seed and chop 1 large, organic tomato. Place in a food processor and process until very smooth. Transfer to a small saucepan; cook, uncovered, over low heat, stirring often, until reduced by half and very thick. Take care not to burn.

Slow-cooker times can vary greatly depending on their age, type and size. Due to the toughness of stew meat, cooking this recipe on High is not recommended; Low temperature settings allow the meat to become tender.

Seafood Stew (Cioppino)

Although it sounds like authentic Italian fare, Cioppino actually traces its roots to the docks of San Francisco. Remember to buy wild-caught fish and seafood whenever possible. This hearty stew can easily be personalized by omitting or adding any type of seafood you like; adjust cooking times accordingly.

Serves: 10

Ingredients:

3/4 cup clarified butter

2 cups chopped onion

3 cloves fresh garlic, minced

1/2 cup fresh organic parsley, minced

2 bottles (8 ounces each) clam juice

2 cans (14 1/2 ounces each) diced tomatoes, undrained

2 dried bay leaves

1 1/2 cups water or homemade fish or chicken stock

4 cans (6.5 ounces each) chopped clams, drained

1 1/2 pounds raw, peeled, de-veined shrimp

3 pounds fish fillets of choice, cut into 1 1/2 inch pieces

1 1/2 cups crab meat, flaked

2 tablespoons fresh basil, chopped

1 tablespoon fresh thyme, chopped

1 tablespoon fresh oregano, chopped

Sea salt to taste

Freshly cracked black pepper to taste

Preparation

In a large stockpot over medium heat, cook onion, garlic and parsley, stirring occasionally, until translucent. Add clam juice, tomatoes, bay leaves and water or stock. Bring to a boil; reduce heat and simmer, covered, for 45 to 60 minutes.

Add clams, shrimp, fish, crab, basil, thyme and oregano. Bring back to a boil and simmer, covered, for 10 minutes or until shrimp are fully cooked (opaque). Discard bay leaves before serving.

Broiled Lamb Chops with Fresh Mint Pesto

Simple yet impressive, this dish is as appropriate for guests as it is for a weeknight family dinner! For those who can tolerate **seeds***.*

Serves: 4

Ingredients:

4 organic, grass-fed lamb chops (2 pounds total)

Sea salt and freshly cracked black pepper to taste

1/4 cup pine nuts, toasted

3 cloves fresh garlic

1 1/2 cups fresh organic basil, chopped

3/4 cup fresh organic mint leaves, chopped

1/4 cup organic olive oil, extra-virgin

As desired: sea salt, fresh lemon juice and freshly cracked black pepper

1 pound fresh organic asparagus spears, washed, trimmed and cut into 2-inch pieces

Fresh lemon wedges (for serving)

Clarified butter (for serving)

Preparation

Preheat your broiler and lightly grease or oil a baking sheet. Season chops on all sides with salt and pepper. Place chops under boiler, approximately 4 inches from heat. Broil for 5 to 8 minutes per side or until desired doneness is reached (see Note).

While chops cook, process pine nuts and garlic in a food processor until chopped. Add fresh basil and mint; process until combined. Add olive oil; process until desired texture is reached. Season to taste with salt, lemon juice and pepper.

In a large saucepan, bring lightly salted water to a boil. Blanch the asparagus by submerging and cooking for 3 to 5 minutes, or until crisp-tender and color has brightened.

Serve each chop topped with pesto, alongside blanched asparagus with lemon wedges and butter. .

Bison Steaks with Mushrooms and Bacon

Bison is nearly always responsibly raised, making it an excellent alternative to industrially-raised beef. However, if you can't find bison at your supermarket, you may substitute organic, grass-fed beef steaks.

Serves: 4

Ingredients:

3 strips organic bacon, chopped

4 organic, grass-fed bison steaks (1 pound total)

Sea salt and freshly cracked black pepper to taste

4 tablespoons clarified butter

1 pound fresh organic button mushrooms, sliced

1 bag (16 ounces) frozen California-mix vegetable blend (broccoli, carrots and cauliflower)

Additional clarified butter (for serving)

Preparation

Preheat your oven to 400 degrees.

In a large, oven-proof skillet over medium heat, cook bacon until crisp. Drain and set aside, reserving 3 tablespoons drippings.

Season bison steaks with salt and pepper. In same skillet over medium heat, cook bison steaks in 2 tablespoon of drippings until browned. If desired doneness is not reached, place skillet with steaks in the oven, top with 1 tablespoon butter each and cook until done (see Note).

While bison is cooking, sauté mushrooms in remaining 1 tablespoon drippings until golden brown and tender. Return bacon to pan and combine.

In a large microwave-safe dish, place vegetable blend and 1/2 cup *water*. Place in microwave, partially cover and cook on high until tender. Toss with butter.

Serve each bison steak with mushroom-bacon mixture spooned on top, alongside vegetable blend.

Notes:

Bison doneness temperatures, using an instant-read meat thermometer:

Medium: 145 to 150 degrees
Medium-Well: 155 degrees
Well-Done: 165 to 170 degrees and up

Zesty Grilled Chicken and Vegetables

This light yet satisfying southwest-spiced recipe lets you enjoy grilled flavor during cold months when outdoor cooking is not an option!

Serves: 4

Ingredients:

4 organic, free-range boneless, skinless chicken breasts (1 pound total)

Sea salt and freshly cracked black pepper, to taste

1 tablespoon light-flavored olive oil

3/4 cup clarified

1 tablespoon fresh organic chives, chopped

1/4 teaspoon cumin

1/8 teaspoon cayenne

1/8 teaspoon chili powder

1 bag (16 ounces) stir-fry vegetable blend (bell peppers and onions)

Preparation

In a large zippered plastic bag, pound chicken breasts to uniform 1/2 inch thickness. Discard bag

Heat a grill pan over medium heat on stove burner. When pan is ready, add oil and chicken. Cook approximately 4 minutes per side, or until no longer pink and cooked through (165 degrees). Remove from pan and set aside.

In a small bowl, thoroughly combine butter with chives, cumin, cayenne and chili powder. Brush a small amount of flavored butter onto hot chicken breasts.

In a large, microwave-safe dish, place vegetable blend and 1/2 cup *water*. Cook on high until vegetables are crisp-tender. Toss with remaining flavored butter and serve alongside seasoned chicken breasts.

Notes:

Flattening chicken breasts helps them to cook uniformly, eliminating under-cooked and over-cooked spots.

Flavored butters, also known as compound butters, are an easy way to add big flavor to any dish. Experiment to create your own blends!

Classic Pork Chop Supper

The timeless pairing of pork chops and apples is translated into a protein- and vegetable-packed dinner with loads of kid appeal!

Serves: 4

Ingredients:

4 organic, boneless pork chops (approximately 1 pound total)

1/8 teaspoon cumin

1/8 teaspoon dried sage, crushed

1/8 teaspoon dried mustard

Sea salt and freshly cracked black pepper, to taste

1 tablespoon clarified butter

2 cups shredded organic red cabbage

1 organic carrot, peeled and shredded

1 organic apple, washed and cut into strips

1/4 cup fresh onion, diced

1/2 cup raisins

4 tablespoons organic olive oil, extra-virgin

1 tablespoon vinegar (approximately, to taste)

1/4 teaspoon chili powder

1/4 teaspoon cumin

1/4 teaspoon cayenne

Sea salt and freshly cracked black pepper

1 cup unsweetened applesauce, heated if desired, for serving

Ground cinnamon for garnish, if desired

Preparation

Preheat your oven to 400 degrees.

Season chops with cumin, sage, mustard, salt and pepper as desired. In a large oven-proof skillet over medium heat, cook chops in butter until nicely browned on both sides. Transfer skillet to oven and cook until desired doneness is reached (see Note).

Meanwhile, in a large bowl, combine cabbage, apple, onion and raisins. Drizzle on olive oil; toss to coat thoroughly. Add vinegar to taste and seasonings; combine thoroughly.

Top each chop with 1/4 cup applesauce and cinnamon, alongside prepared slaw.

Note:

USDA recommendations recently changed the safe temperature of cooked pork to 145 degrees. However, if you dislike a pink appearance, cook until internal temperature registers 160 degrees.

Easy Stuffed Chicken Breasts with Spring Vegetables

*While the idea of a stuffed chicken breast seems difficult, this fresh-tasting dish makes it easy and fast! If Swiss cheese is used, this recipe is suitable for those who can tolerate **dairy**.*

Serves: 6

Ingredients:

6 organic, free-range chicken breasts (approximately 3 1/2 pounds)

1 pound organic spinach, washed and coarsely chopped

2 cloves fresh garlic, minced

5 tablespoons clarified butter, divided

6 slices deli ham, low-salt, no MSG, sulfites or carrageenan

6 thin slices Swiss cheese (if desired)

1 1/2 cups fresh organic asparagus, washed, trimmed and cut into 1 1/2 inch pieces

1 1/2 cups fresh organic green beans, washed, trimmed and cut into 1 1/2 inch pieces

1 cup fresh or frozen organic green peas

Prepared mustard (for serving)

Lemon wedges (for serving)

Preparation

Preheat oven to 400 degrees; lightly grease a baking sheet.

In a large skillet over low heat, cook spinach and garlic in 2 tablespoons butter until spinach is wilted.

In a large plastic zipper bag, pound chicken breasts to 1/2 inch thickness; discard bag.

Place 1 slice of ham atop each chicken breast; top with 1/4 cup spinach mixture. Fold in half to cover filling; secure with toothpicks to seal. Place on prepared baking sheet and bake approximately 30 minutes, until no pink remains and chicken is cooked through (165 degrees).

Meanwhile, place asparagus, green beans and peas in a large microwave-safe dish with 1/2 cup *water*. Place in microwave, partially cover and cook on high until crisp-tender. Toss with remaining 3 tablespoons butter.

Plate each chicken breast alongside steamed vegetables; remove toothpicks. If desired, spoon mustard over each breast or serve on the side. Place a lemon wedge on each plate for dressing vegetables, if desired.

Bright Lemon Chicken with Olives and Arugula

Refreshing and light, this dish is ideal for warm-weather dinners. Paired with a flavorful and seed-free pesto-inspired sauce, the spicy arugula is a perfect compliment.

Ingredients:

Serves: 4

3 pounds organic, free-range chicken pieces, with bones and skin

Sea salt and freshly cracked black pepper to taste

4 tablespoons organic olive oil, extra-virgin, divided

1/2 cup fresh organic basil leaves

2 cloves fresh garlic, peeled

4 cups fresh organic arugula, washed and patted dry

1 fresh organic lemon, cut into thin slices

1/4 cup organic Kalamata olives, pitted, drained

Preparation

Preheat your oven to 400 degrees; lightly oil or grease a baking sheet.

Season the chicken with salt and pepper. In a large skillet over medium-high heat, brown chicken in 1 tablespoon olive oil. Work in batches if necessary. Transfer to baking sheet and bake for approximately 30 minutes, or until no pink remains and thickest pieces of chicken are cooked through (165 degrees).

Meanwhile, place basil leaves and garlic in a food processor. Process until finely chopped. Gradually add the remaining olive oil by teaspoonfuls, pulsing after each addition, until desired consistency is reached. Toss thoroughly with arugula in a large bowl.

In the skillet used to brown chicken, reduce heat to medium and cook lemon slices and olives in drippings until lightly browned, approximately 2 minutes per side.

Divide the chicken and dressed arugula between four plates; top chicken with sautéed lemons and olives.

Note:

If you and your family tolerate nuts and seeds, you may used a prepared pesto sauce in place of the basil, garlic and olive oil mixture.

North African Lamb Stew

Exotic-sounding but a snap to make, this flavorful stew is great for introducing your family to global flavors!

Serves: 4

Ingredients:

3 Roma tomatoes, seeded and chopped

1 pound organic, grass-fed ground lamb

2 teaspoons plus 2 tablespoons olive oil, extra-virgin, divided

2 cups chopped onion

1/2 cup sliced fresh organic carrot

3/4 teaspoon freshly-grated cinnamon (or good-quality ground)

1/2 teaspoon ground coriander

1/4 teaspoon ground red pepper

3/4 teaspoon ground cumin

1 1/2 cups homemade chicken stock

1/2 cup raisins (traditional or golden)

1 1/2 tablespoons freshly grated lemon zest

1/4 teaspoon sea salt

1/4 cup fresh organic cilantro, chopped

4 tablespoons freshly-squeezed lemon juice, divided

1 pound organic baby spinach leaves, washed and patted dry

Preparation

In a food processor, puree tomatoes; set aside.

In a large skillet over medium-high heat, brown and crumble lamb until no pink remains (approximately 7 minutes). Remove from pan and set aside; discard drippings.

In the same pan, heat olive oil; cook onion and carrot approximately 4 minutes. Add seasonings; stir-fry an additional 30 seconds to combine flavors.

Add the chicken stock, raisins, lemon zest, tomato puree, salt and reserved cooked lamb to skillet. Bring to boiling; reduce heat and simmer approximately 5 minutes or until mixture has thickened as desired.

In a large bowl, toss baby spinach leaves with remaining lemon juice and remaining olive oil; divide between four plates. Serve the stew either atop or alongside greens.

Oven-Baked Chicken Stew with Eggplant

Easy to prepare and perfect for chilly evenings, this oven stew is a great way to introduce kids to eggplant!

Serves: 6 to 8

Ingredients:

3 pounds organic, free-range chicken pieces, bone-in, skin on

3 tablespoons clarified butter

2 cups homemade chicken stock

1 large organic eggplant, trimmed and flesh cut into 2-inch pieces

2 fresh organic carrots, washed, trimmed and cut into 2-inch pieces

2 medium red onions, cut into 2-inch wedges

2 stalks fresh organic celery, washed and cut into 2-inch pieces

1 can (14.5 ounces) crushed tomatoes, undrained

3 cloves fresh garlic, minced

1 1/2 teaspoons sea salt

1/2 teaspoon freshly cracked black pepper

1 teaspoon dried sage, crushed (see Note)

1 teaspoon dried thyme, crushed

1 teaspoon dried rosemary, crushed

Preparation

Preheat oven to 350 degrees.

In a very large stockpot or Dutch oven, brown chicken on all sides in butter. Add all remaining ingredients.

Cover and bake for approximately 1 1/2 to 2 hours; until vegetables are tender thickest chicken pieces are cooked through (juices will run clear and internal temperature will register at least 165 degrees). If mixture becomes too dry during cooking, add more chicken stock or water as needed.

Note:

Fresh, organic chopped herbs can be substituted for dried. If using fresh herbs, add them during the last 20 minutes of cooking time to preserve their more delicate flavors.

Chicken "Tabbouleh" Salad with Spinach

Traditional tabbouleh is made from buckwheat and may not be tolerated by some individuals. This version, which looks like actual tabbouleh but tastes much fresher, eliminates the worries of grains and gluten!

Serves: 6

Ingredients:

6 1/2 cups fresh cauliflower pieces

Zest of 1 organic lemon

1/3 cup freshly squeezed lemon juice

1 cup diced fresh organic tomato

2 cups diced fresh organic cucumber

1 tablespoon fresh mint, finely chopped

1/2 cup fresh dill, finely chopped

3/4 cup fresh Italian parsley, finely chopped

2 cups organic, free-range chicken, cooked, shredded or cubed

4 tablespoons organic olive oil, extra-virgin

Sea salt and freshly cracked black pepper to taste

Preparation

2 pounds fresh baby spinach leaves, washed, patted dry

In a food processor, process cauliflower (working in batches if necessary) until it resembles fine crumbs. Using a clean and dry cotton towel, wrap up the cauliflower crumbs and twist them to remove as much excess moisture as possible.

In a large bowl, combine cauliflower crumbs with all remaining ingredients except spinach.

Arrange spinach leaves on individual serving plates; top with cauliflower mixture.

Southwestern Pork Stew

Hearty and perfectly spiced, this stew is a great alternative for those who can't tolerate traditional chili with beans!

Serves: 8

Ingredients:

1/4 cup light-flavored olive oil

4 1/2 pounds organic pork shoulder, sliced in 2-inch pieces

Sea salt and freshly ground black pepper to taste

2 cups yellow onions, chopped

3 cups fresh organic carrots, sliced into 2-inch pieces

8 cloves fresh garlic, peeled and finely minced

3 organic poblano peppers, washed, seeded and julienned

1 organic dried ancho chile pepper, seeded, julienned

3 bay leaves

1/8 teaspoon cumin

1/4 cup freshly squeezed lime juice

6 cups homemade chicken stock

1 1/2 cups organic Roma tomatoes, washed, seeded and coarsely chopped

1/4 cup fresh organic cilantro, chopped

Preparation

Lightly season pork with salt and pepper. In a very large stockpot or Dutch oven over medium heat, thoroughly brown pork in oil (work in 2 batches; approximately 10 minutes per batch).

Return all pork to stockpot; add onions, carrots, garlic, both peppers, bay leaves, cumin, lime juice and chicken stock. Bring to a boil.

Reduce heat to a simmer; add tomatoes. Cover and cook until carrots are tender and pork is cooked through; approximately 3 hours. Remove bay leaves before serving.

Easy Italian Beef Stew

Rich and hearty, this stew takes advantage of canned tomatoes and Italian seasoning blend. Prep time is very short, allowing you to assemble the stew and have plenty of spare time while it cooks!

Serves: 6

Ingredients:

1 pound organic, grass-fed beef stew meat, cubed

1 tablespoon extra-virgin olive oil

2 cloves fresh garlic, minced

1 can (14 1/2 ounces) diced tomatoes, drained

1 tablespoon no-sugar-added Italian seasoning blend

3 cups homemade beef stock

1/2 teaspoon dried marjoram, crushed

1/4 teaspoon dried red pepper flakes, crushed

1 (16 ounce) bag frozen stew vegetable blend (onions, carrots and celery) OR 3/4 cup each,

fresh, organic, cubed

Sea salt and freshly cracked black pepper to taste

Preparation

Season the stew meat as desired with salt and pepper. In a very large stockpot or Dutch oven over medium heat, brown stew meat in oil approximately 10 minutes.

Add garlic, tomatoes, Italian seasoning, stock, marjoram and red pepper flakes. Bring to boiling. Reduce heat and simmer, covered, for 1 hour.

Add fresh or frozen vegetables and simmer 1/2 hour longer, or until stew meat is very tender.

Notes:

For small children or those who dislike spicy foods, leave out red pepper flakes.

As with most recipes which call for beef, bison meat can be substituted.

Tuscan Omelet with Fresh Tomato Relish

*Organic, cage-free eggs aren't just for breakfast! Here, these excellent sources of protein get a kick from a cheese-and-garlic filling and flavorful fresh herbed tomato sauce. For those who can tolerate **dairy** and **eggs**.* Serves: 4

Ingredients:

1 cup organic, fresh tomato, seeded and chopped

1/4 cup fresh organic scallions, thinly sliced

2 tablespoons fresh organic basil, chopped

2 tablespoons fresh organic oregano, chopped

1 pound organic baby spinach leaves, washed and patted dry

2 cloves fresh garlic, minced

3 tablespoons clarified butter, divided

8 organic, cage-free eggs

2 tablespoons organic whole milk

Sea salt and freshly cracked black pepper to taste

1 cup shredded organic mozzarella cheese

1/4 cup freshly grated Parmesan cheese

Preparation

In a small bowl, combine tomato, scallions, basil and oregano; set aside.

In a large skillet over medium heat, sauté garlic in 1 tablespoon butter until softened, approximately 1 minute. Add spinach; cook, stirring constantly, until spinach is cooked and wilted. Set aside.

In another large (10 inch) nonstick skillet, heat 1 tablespoon butter over medium heat. In a large bowl, whisk together eggs, milk, salt and pepper until well-combined and color has lightened (you may also use an electric hand mixer on low speed).

Pour half of egg mixture into prepared skillet. Cook for 2 minutes; stir to allow uncooked portion to flow under cooked portion. Cook another 3 to 4 minutes or until eggs are set and cooked through (165 degrees). Repeat with remaining egg mixture and butter.

To assemble omelets, divide spinach mixture between both; sprinkle with 1/2 cup mozzarella cheese each and fold omelets over filling. Top with reserved tomato-herb mixture to serve.

Roast Beef with Root Vegetable Blend

Roasting root vegetables allows their flavors to intensify, creating a whole new twist on an old favorite! Serves 4

Ingredients:

1 (3 pound) organic, grass-fed tri-tip sirloin beef roast

Sea salt and freshly cracked black pepper to taste

1 pound fresh organic beets, greens removed, peeled and cut in 1 1/2 inch pieces

1 large organic sweet potato, peeled, cut in 1 1/2 inch pieces

1 large organic parsnip, peeled, cut in 1 1/2 inch pieces

6 organic carrots, greens removed, peeled, cut in 1 1/2 inch pieces

1 red onion, cut into 1 1/2 inch wedges

8 fresh cloves garlic, whole

1 tablespoon dried thyme, crushed

1 tablespoon dried rosemary, crushed

3 tablespoons organic olive oil, extra-virgin

Sea salt and freshly cracked black pepper to taste

Preparation

Preheat your oven to 425 degrees. Place a rack into a roasting pan. Line a rimmed baking sheet with aluminum foil.

Rub the roast with salt and pepper as desired; place in rack.

In a large bowl, combine beets, sweet potato, parsnip, carrots, onion, garlic, thyme, rosemary and olive oil; toss well to coat thoroughly. Season with salt and pepper to taste. Arrange the vegetable mixture on prepared pan in a single layer, leaving room between individual pieces.

Place one oven rack in top third of oven and another rack in bottom third.

Place the beef roast on upper oven rack; place baking sheet with vegetables on lower rack. Roast, stirring vegetables after 20 minutes, until meat is done (see Note) and vegetables are golden-brown and tender. If the roast begins to brown too quickly, loosely tent with aluminum foil.

To serve, slice approximately 6 ounces of beef per person; plate with roasted vegetables.

Note: Temperatures for beef doneness, using an instant-read meat thermometer:

Medium: 145 to 150 degrees
Medium-Well: 155 degrees
Well-Done: 165 to 170 degrees and up

Chapter 4

Snacks

Tasty Treats

Ultra-Simple Parmesan Crisps

*Incredibly easy to make, these crisps are great as a snack or served at parties. While still warm, try shaping them over shot glasses to make 'cups' for filling! For those who can tolerate **dairy**.*

Serves: Varies

Ingredients:

1 cup good-quality Parmesan cheese (see Note)

1/8 teaspoon garlic powder

1/8 teaspoon onion powder

<u>Preparation</u>

Preheat your oven to 325 degrees. Line a baking sheet with a silicone baking mat.

In a small bowl, combine Parmesan and seasonings. Spoon onto prepared baking sheet, flattening to create the size of crisp you prefer. Leave plenty of room for spreading.

Bake until cheese is melted, flattened and barely browned; approximately 5 minutes. Watch crisps throughout the cooking process to prevent burning; they melt very quickly.

Note: Canned or jarred varieties of Parmesan will not work in this recipe; their texture is too dry.

Crispy Kale Chips

A wonderful alternative to the refined carbs and questionable oils in store-bought potato chips, these healthy snacks couldn't be simpler to prepare!

Serves: Varies

Ingredients:

1 pound organic Tuscan kale, thoroughly washed and patted dry

1 tablespoon organic extra-virgin olive oil

1/2 teaspoon sea salt

1/2 teaspoon freshly cracked black pepper

1/4 teaspoon garlic powder

<u>Preparation</u>

Preheat your oven to 350 degrees; lightly grease or oil a baking sheet.

Press dried kale between paper towels, removing as much excess moisture as possible. The drier your kale is before baking, the crisper the resulting chips will be.

In a large bowl, toss kale with olive oil, salt, pepper and garlic powder to coat.

Arrange in a single layer on prepared baking sheet. Bake for 5 to 7 minutes, checking after 4 minutes, until kale is crispy.

Note:

Although the seasonings listed here create a very tasty chip, these chips combine wonderfully with virtually any seasoning combination you enjoy. Experiment and create your own blend!

Garlic and Herb Flaxseed Crackers

*A great alternative to purchased crackers made with refined grains, these crispy snacks are suitable for those who can tolerate **dairy** and **seeds**.*

Serves: Varies

Ingredients:

1 cup organic ground flaxseed meal

1/3 cup freshly grated organic Parmesan cheese (not jarred)

1 teaspoon dried basil, crushed

1 teaspoon dried rosemary, crushed

1 teaspoon dried oregano, crushed

1/4 teaspoon sea salt

1/2 teaspoon freshly cracked black pepper

1/2 cup water

Preparation

Preheat your oven to 400 degrees. Line a baking sheet with waxed paper or a silicone baking mat.

In a small bowl, combine all ingredients; stir to mix well.

Spread approximately 1/8 inch thick onto prepared baking sheet, leveling carefully to ensure there are no thin or thick spots. Thinner spots will burn, while thicker spots will under-cook.

Bake for approximately 15 to 19 minutes, checking after 12 minutes, until golden brown and crispy. Remove from oven; let stand until cooled. Break into cracker-sized pieces.

Note:

Feel free to substitute any herbs, spices or seasoning blends you like in this recipe for a world of potential variations! If you choose a mixture which does not go well with Parmesan cheese, leave the cheese out and increase flaxseed meal by 1/3 cup.

Smoky Deviled Eggs with Bacon

*As delicious as a snack as they are as a party appetizer, these decadent eggs are suitable for those who can tolerate **dairy** and **eggs**.*

Serves: Varies

Work Time: 10 minutes

Total Time: 10 minutes, plus chilling

Ingredients:

12 organic, cage-free eggs, hard-boiled, peeled

3 strips organic bacon, chopped

Clarified butter, as needed

1/3 cup olive-oil mayo (see recipe for Sweet Potato Salad with Pork)

3/4 teaspoon dried mustard

1/4 teaspoon smoked paprika

2 tablespoons freshly snipped chives, divided

Sea salt and freshly cracked black pepper to taste

Preparation

In a skillet over medium heat, cook bacon until crisp. Drain on paper towels. Measure drippings; add butter if needed to reach 2 tablespoons.

Cut eggs in half; place yolks into a small bowl. Add the drippings, butter (if used), mayo, mustard, paprika, 1 tablespoon chives and salt and pepper to taste. Combine and mash until mixture is smooth.

Spoon yolk mixture back into eggs, sprinkle with remaining chives and refrigerate, covered, until serving.

Portobello Mushrooms with Avocado Chicken Stuffing

*Satisfying and hearty any time of day, this different twist on stuffed mushrooms can be easily modified for those who don't like or can't tolerate **dairy** or **seeds** (see Note).*   Serves: Varies

Ingredients:

16 small organic portobello mushrooms, washed, gills and stems removed

1/4 cup clarified butter

2 1/2 cups red onion, chopped

2 cloves fresh garlic, finely minced

1 1/2 cups organic, free-range chicken, cooked, shredded

4 large organic avocados (8 ounces each), peeled, cored and chopped

1/4 cup fresh organic cilantro, chopped

2 tablespoons freshly squeezed lime juice

1/8 teaspoon ground cumin

1/8 teaspoon chili powder

1/2 teaspoon sea salt

1/2 teaspoon freshly cracked black pepper

1 (8 ounce) package cream cheese, at room temperature

1/4 cup plus 2 tablespoons pepitas (pumpkin seeds) (optional)

4 tablespoons organic olive oil, extra-virgin

Additional lime juice, if desired, for garnish

Additional chopped cilantro, if desired, for garnish

Preparation

Preheat your oven to 400 degrees; lightly oil a baking sheet.

In a large skillet over medium heat, sauté onion and garlic in butter until translucent and soft.

In a mixing bowl, combine chicken, avocado, cilantro, lime juice, cumin, chili powder, salt and pepper. Combine, mashing thoroughly to desired consistency.

Place the mushroom caps on prepared baking sheet; divide cream cheese among caps. Top with avocado mixture; sprinkle with pepitas, if desired. Drizzle caps with olive oil.

Bake caps for 5 minutes; loosely tent with aluminum foil and bake another 3 to 5 minutes or until heated through. Serve caps hot, with additional lime juice and cilantro if desired.

Notes: These stuffed mushrooms are just as delicious without the additions of cream cheese and pepitas (toasted pumpkin seeds); no recipe adjustments necessary.

Crispy Oven Party Wings with Cajun-Butter Dipping Sauce

Traditional wing recipes often rely on dairy-based dipping sauces or those with added sugars. These deliciously different wings crisp up beautifully in the oven and are sure to be a huge hit at your next party!

Serves: 12 to 20, depending on serving size

Ingredients:

5 pounds organic, free-range chicken wings, prepped (see Note)

2 tablespoons light-flavored organic olive oil

2 teaspoons sea salt

1 teaspoon freshly cracked black pepper

Dipping Sauce:

1 cup clarified butter

1/2 teaspoon sea salt

1/2 teaspoon freshly cracked black pepper

1/2 teaspoon dried thyme, crushed

1/2 teaspoon smoked paprika

1/8 teaspoon onion powder

1/2 teaspoon garlic powder

1/2 teaspoon dried oregano, crushed

1/4 teaspoon red pepper flakes, crushed (optional)

1/8 teaspoon cayenne pepper (optional)

Preparation

To prepare wings, preheat oven to 400 degrees. Place wire roasting racks inside 2 baking sheets; lightly grease racks. Line sheets with foil, if desired, to make cleanup easier.

Place wings, in a single layer, on prepared racks. Bake wings until golden brown, crispy and cooked through (165 degrees); approximately 45 to 50 minutes.

To prepare dipping sauce, thoroughly combine butter and all seasonings. Serve wings on a platter with dipping sauce in the center, or provide individual-size cups of dipping sauce for each diner.

Note:

Chicken wings can be baked as-is. However, some simple tricks like separating the drumettes from the flats and trimming the tips will enhance your final product. Your butcher will know how to do this.

Bacon-Wrapped Shrimp with Garlic-Butter Dipping Sauce

Ideal for cookouts or parties, this delicious and savory shrimp recipe can also be cooked on an outdoor grill!

Serves: 12 (approximately)

Ingredients:

40 strips organic thin-cut bacon (see Note)

40 large responsibly-farmed shrimp, peeled and de-veined

3/4 cup clarified butter

1/4 teaspoon crushed red pepper flakes (optional)

1 teaspoon garlic powder

Preparation

Preheat your broiler. Line 2 large baking sheets with aluminum foil; grease the foil.

In a large skillet over medium heat (working in batches if necessary), cook bacon to half-doneness. Remove and drain on paper towels.

Wrap each bacon slice around a shrimp, securing with soaked wooden toothpicks (see note). Place on prepared baking sheets and broil approximately 5 minutes. Flip and broil another 4 minutes or until cooked through (at least 145 degrees) and thickest parts of shrimp are opaque. Remove from oven.

While shrimp are broiling, combing butter, red pepper flakes if desired and garlic powder in a small bowl.

To serve, arrange shrimp on a platter with dipping sauce in center or give each diner their own individual-size container of sauce. Serve shrimp immediately after removing from oven.

Notes:

Purchasing thinner bacon ensures that both bacon and shrimp will cook at the same speed.

Soaking wooden toothpicks in water ensures that the toothpicks will not burn during cooking.

To Grill: Working on a well-oiled grate, grill shrimp for the same amount of time as under a broiler, watching carefully to avoid flare-ups and burning.

Chapter 5

Additional
Resources

More Goodness

Other Popular Best Selling Cookbooks For Kindle and Print

We have listed both the short titles and the full titles of these books to make them easier to locate.

You can also search Amazon.com for "best selling cookbooks 2012" or "best selling cookbooks 2013" for an up to date listing.

Other Books by New Health CookBooks

Fat Chance CookBook: The Low Sugar High Fiber Cookbook – 40 Delicious & Healthy Recipes That Your Family Will Love by New Health CookBooks

My Virgin Diet CookBook: The Gluten-Free, Soy-Free, Egg-Free, Dairy-Free, Peanut-Free, Corn-Free and Sugar-Free Cookbook by Rebecca Lorraine

Cookbooks by Other Authors

Cooking Light Cookbook by Cooking Light

Cooking Light The Essential Dinner Tonight Cookbook: Over 350 Delicious, Easy, and Healthy Meals by Cooking Light

Forks Over Knives Cookbook by Del Sroufe

Forks Over Knives-The Cookbook: Over 300 Recipes for Plant-Based Eating All Through the Year by Del Sroufe

The Low Blood Sugar Cookbook by Patricia Krimmel, Edward Krimmel

The Low Blood Sugar Cookbook: Sugarless Cooking for Everyone by Patricia Krimmel, Edward Krimmel

The Blood Sugar Solution Cookbook by Mark Hyman

The Blood Sugar Solution Cookbook: More than 175 Ultra-Tasty Recipes for Total Health and Weight Loss by Mark Hyman

Eat What You Love by Marlene Koch

Eat What You Love: More than 300 Incredible Recipes Low in Sugar, Fat, and Calories by Marlene Koch

From Mama's Table to Mine by Bobby Deen

From Mama's Table to Mine: Everybody's Favorite Comfort Foods at 350 Calories or Less by Bobby Deen

Gather, the Art of Paleo Entertaining by Bill Staley and Hayley Mason

It's All Good by Gwyneth Paltrow

It's All Good: Delicious, Easy Recipes That Will Make You Look Good and Feel Great by Gwyneth Paltrow

Jumpstart to Skinny: The Simple 3-Week Plan for

Supercharged Weight Loss by Bob Harper and Greg Critser

My Beef with Meat by Rip Esselstyn

My Beef with Meat: The Healthiest Argument for Eating a Plant-Strong Diet--Plus 140 New Engine 2 Recipes by Rip Esselstyn

Nourishing Traditions by Sally Fallon

Nourishing Traditions: The Cookbook that Challenges Politically Correct Nutrition and the Diet Dictocrats by Sally Fallon

Practical Paleo by Diane Sanfilippo

Practical Paleo: A Customized Approach to Health and a Whole-Foods Lifestyle by Diane Sanfilippo

Primal Blueprint Quick and Easy Meals by Mark Sisson and Jennifer Meier

Primal Blueprint Quick and Easy Meals: Delicious, Primal-approved meals you can make in under 30 minutes by Mark Sisson and Jennifer Meier

Relish by Daphne Oz

Relish: An Adventure in Food, Style, and Everyday Fun by Daphne Oz

Superfood Smoothies by Julie Morris

Superfood Smoothies: 100 Delicious, Energizing & Nutrient-dense Recipes by Julie Morris

The America's Test Kitchen Healthy Family Cookbook by America's Test Kitchen

The America's Test Kitchen Healthy Family Cookbook: A New, Healthier Way to Cook Everything from America's Most Trusted Test Kitchen by America's Test Kitchen

The Biggest Loser Cookbook by Devin Alexander and Karen Kaplan

The Biggest Loser Cookbook: More Than 125 Healthy, Delicious Recipes Adapted from NBC's Hit Show by Devin Alexander and Karen Kaplan

The Fresh 20 by Melissa Lanz

The Fresh 20: 20-Ingredient Meal Plans for Health and Happiness 5 Nights a Week by Melissa Lanz

The Mediterranean Diet Cookbook by Rockridge University Press

The Mediterranean Diet Cookbook: A Mediterranean Cookbook with 150 Healthy Mediterranean Diet Recipes by Rockridge University Press

The Paleo Diet Cookbook by Loren Cordain and Nell Stephenson

The Paleo Diet Cookbook: More Than 150 Recipes for

Paleo Breakfasts, Lunches, Dinners, Snacks, and Beverages by Loren Cordain and Nell Stephenson

What's for Dinner? by Curtis Stone

What's for Dinner?: Delicious Recipes for a Busy Life by Curtis Stone

Wheat Belly Cookbook by William Davis MD

Wheat Belly Cookbook: 150 Recipes to Help You Lose the Wheat, Lose the Weight, and Find Your Path Back to Health by William Davis MD

Weight Loss Books And Diet Books

You can also search for "weight loss books best sellers 2012" or "weight loss best sellers 2013" for a current list.

The Atkins Diet

Dr. Atkins' New Diet Revolution by Robert C. Atkins

Cooked by Michael Pollan

Cooked: A Natural History of Transformation by Michael Pollan

Eat to Live by Joel Fuhrman

Eat to Live: The Amazing Nutrient-Rich Program for Fast and Sustained Weight Loss by Joel Fuhrman

Fat Chance by Robert H. Lustig

Fat Chance: Beating the Odds Against Sugar, Processed Food, Obesity, and Disease by Robert H. Lustig

Good Calories, Bad Calories by Gary Taubes

The Blood Sugar Solution by Mark Hyman

The Blood Sugar Solution: The UltraHealthy Program for Losing Weight, Preventing Disease, and Feeling Great Now! by Mark Hyman

The 5:2 Diet Book by Kate Harrison

The 5:2 Diet Book: Feast for 5 Days a Week and Fast for 2 to Lose Weight, Boost Your Brain and Transform Your Health by Kate Harrison

The Five Two Diet Book

The Art and Science of Low Carbohydrate Living by Stephen Phinney and Jeff Volek

The Art and Science of Low Carbohydrate Living: An Expert Guide to Making the Life-Saving Benefits of Carbohydrate Restriction Sustainable and Enjoyable by Stephen Phinney, Jeff Volek

The Fast Diet by Michael Mosley and Mimi Spencer

The Fast Diet: Lose Weight, Stay Healthy, and Live Longer with the Simple Secret of Intermittent Fasting by Michael Mosley and Mimi Spencer

The Fast Metabolism Diet by Haylie Pomroy

The Fast Metabolism Diet: Eat More Food and Lose More Weight by Haylie Pomroy

The New Atkins for a New You by Dr. Eric C. Westman, Dr. Stephen D. Phinney, Jeff S. Volek

The Paleo Solution by Robb Wolf

The Paleo Solution: The Original Human Diet by Robb Wolf, or Rob Wolf
Wheat Belly by William Davis MD

Wheat Belly: Lose the Wheat, Lose the Weight, and Find Your Path Back To Health by William Davis MD

The Primal Blueprint by Mark Sisson

The Primal Blueprint: Reprogram your genes for effortless weight loss, vibrant health and boundless energy by Mark Sisson

The Healthy Green Drink Diet by Jason Manheim

The Healthy Green Drink Diet: Advice and Recipes to Energize, Alkalize, Lose Weight, and Feel Great by Jason Manheim

Forks Over Knives by Gene Stone

Forks Over Knives: The Plant-Based Way to Health by Gene Stone

Deadly Harvest by Geoff Bond

Deadly Harvest: The Intimate Relationship Between Our Heath and Our Food by Geoff Bond

The Rosedale Diet by Ron Rosedale and Carol Colman

Ignore the awkward by Uffe Ravnskov

Ignore the awkward! How the cholesterol myths are kept alive by Uffe Ravnskov

Primal Body, Primal Mind by Nora Gedgaudas

Primal Body, Primal Mind: Beyond the Paleo Diet for Total Health and a Longer Life by Nora T. Gedgaudas, CNS, CNT

Deep Nutrition by Catherine Shanahan

Deep Nutrition: Why Your Genes Need Traditional Food by Catherine Shanahan MD

The Skinny Rules by Bob Harper

The Skinny Rules: The Simple, Nonnegotiable Principles for Getting to Thin by Bob Harper

Protein Power by Dr. Eades

Protein Power: The High-Protein/Low-Carbohydrate Way to Lose Weight, Feel Fit, and Boost Your Health--in Just Weeks! by Michael R. Eades, Mary Dan Eades

Eat to Live by Dr. Joel Fuhrman

Eat to Live: The Amazing Nutrient-Rich Program for Fast and Sustained Weight Loss by Joel Fuhrman

The Paleo Answer by Loren Cordain

The Paleo Answer: 7 Days to Lose Weight, Feel Great, Stay Young by Loren Cordain

The Seventeen Day Diet by Mike Moreno

The 17 Day Diet by Mike Moreno

The China Study by T. Colin Campbell

The China Study: The Most Comprehensive Study of Nutrition Ever Conducted And the Startling Implications for Diet by T. Colin Campbell

Choose to Lose by Chris Powell

Choose to Lose: The 7-Day Carb Cycle Solution by Chris Powell

Fit2Fat2Fit by Drew Manning

Fit2Fat2Fit: The Unexpected Lessons from Gaining and

Losing 75 lbs on Purpose by Drew Manning

The Belly Fat Diet by John Chatham

The Belly Fat Diet: Lose Your Belly, Shed Excess Weight, Improve Health by John Chatham

The Dukan Diet Book by Pierre Dukan

The Dukan Diet: 2 Steps to Lose the Weight, 2 Steps to Keep It Off Forever by Pierre Dukan

The Mayo Clinic Diet Book

The Mayo Clinic Diet: Eat Well, Enjoy Life, Lose Weight by Mayo Clinic

The Mayo Clinic Diabetes Diet by Mayo Clinic

The Virgin Diet by JJ Virgin

The Virgin Diet: Drop 7 Foods, Lose 7 Pounds, Just 7 Days by JJ Virgin

101 Best Foods to Boost Your Metabolism by Metabolic-Calculator.com

Pure Fat Burning Fuel by Isabel De Los Rios

Pure Fat Burning Fuel: Follow This Simple, Heart Healthy Path To Total Fat Loss by Isabel De Los Rios

It Starts with Food by Melissa Hartwig

It Starts with Food: Discover the Whole30 and Change Your Life in Unexpected Ways by Melissa Hartwig

Shred by Ian K. Smith

Shred: The Revolutionary Diet: 6 Weeks 4 Inches 2 Sizes by Ian K. Smith

The Four Hour Body by Timothy Ferriss

The 4-Hour Body: The Secrets and Science of Rapid Body Transformation by Timothy Ferriss

VB6 by Mark Bittman

VB6: Eat Vegan Before 6:00 to Lose Weight and Restore Your Health . . . for Good by Mark Bittman

VB6: Eat Vegan Before 6:00 to Lose Weight and Restore Your Health . . . for Good by Mark Bittman

Wheat Belly by William Davis MD

Wheat Belly: Lose the Wheat, Lose the Weight, and Find Your Path Back To Health by William Davis MD

Why We Get Fat by Gary Taubes

Why We Get Fat: And What to Do About It by Gary Taubes

25744882R00062

Made in the USA
Lexington, KY
02 September 2013